climbing

in the

dark

> Dearest Debbie
> My climb began at a circle of appreciation you created & held with gentle strength. I am forever grateful for having you in my life.
> Adeola x

adeola sheehy-adekale

"This is the one, the poetry book to read if you are on the path of reclaiming yourself after an end. Adeola, after a 20-year relationship ending, shares her experience on life after this end. We feel the sorrow, the rage, the regrets, the what ifs poured onto the pages. We also feel the hope, the yearning, and the rediscovery of herself in this new beginning. She tells her story eloquently, passionately, and with full vulnerability. I adored the journey she took me on and cannot wait for you to take it as well."

- *Tania Hart*,
Author of Wild One

"These words resonate so deeply within my soul it's as if I have been exposed on the page. The grief, beauty and strength within this book and the way the words dance across the page is both inspiring and liberating, offering hope even within the darkest times. Delving into this beautiful book will take you on a life changing journey."

- *Kat Shaw*,
Artist

"Climbing in the Dark is a raw, unapologetic and searingly honest portrayal of grief, loneliness and the journey we all take at one time or another to claw our way out of the darkness. Oscillating between emotions, Adeola's poetry beautifully questions why and how we feel so deeply, as her old self flakes away and she awakens into the light."

- Eleanor Cheetham,
Founder of Creative Countryside

"Climbing in the Dark is a beautiful look at honest living. Adeola has an incredible way with words to describe what so many of us walk through without knowing quite how to express ourselves. In each step of this book, Adeola takes us on a journey of heartbreak but also strength. And in the end, she leaves us full of hope and renewal."

- Sarah Hartley,
Creator of The Kindred Voice

"This poetry collection is really a travelogue, because in takes the reader on a tumultuous journey. The author's pain in the process is palpable. Her exploration of how she had denied herself is a revelation. What a feat of transmutation! This work, these words need to be out in the world. And all of us, whether or not we have gone thru this kind of break up, have taken steps that were not true to us. These poems show us how to find our way back."

- *Gina Martin,*
Author of the When She Wakes
series and WomEnchanting

"A brave and beautiful collection of poems written after the end of a long relationship - each section sees the author climbing slowly out of the darkness, finally emerging into the light knowing who she is, brighter, stronger, more powerful than ever. As each poem reaches for the light, we see trauma dealt with and the determination of the human spirit progressing towards brighter days."

- *Chantelle Atkins,*
Author of The Boy With The
Thorn In His Side series

"A spellbinding journey of a woman becoming. The heartbreak, grief, empowerment, and freedom of self will have you returning again and again to these poems that hurt and heal in equal measure."

- Mia Sutton,
Co-Founder of Illuminate Writing

"Raw and real. Climbing in the Dark comes straight from the heart and catches you unawares."

- Lucy H. Pearce,
Author of Burning Woman

"It's deeply moving to ride the waves with Adeola in Climbing in the Dark. Swimming with the grief, the hope, the self-arrival and power. Each piece offers permission to feel into every emotion expressed. We're invited into a cathartic world of empowerment on every page."

- Leora Leboff,
Menstrual and Menopause Mentor
and co-founder of WomanKind

Thank you to my book doulas

Laura Lewis
Laci Hoyt
Hannah Kewley

Without your support this book would never have come to be, I am more grateful than I could ever say for your friendship.

contents

foreward	2
the fall	5
endings	17
questioning	29
grief	41
here in the quiet	53
reaching in	67
surrender in strength	79
quiet certainty	93
into the light	103
the fires ignite	115

foreward

We get hit with crisis points all too often in our lives. Crossroads moments that feel like they could break us as they change the reality we thought was our solid ground.

The moment my twenty-year relationship ended was one of those moments. It became a catalyst for deepening my connection to myself and embarking on a new path into the future. The darkness was a thick, palpable thing, breathing down my neck and suffocating my voice, so I began to write. Each day I would ask myself only to arrive at the page honestly, to spill my truth and release the emotions and thoughts that threatened to overwhelm me.

Tears and ink mingled and slowly black turned to grey and the dark grew lighter.

For one hundred days I gave myself permission to feel and express. Each day was a step closer to a home whose ground could never be shaken. From the whispers in the dark, to the roar in the sunlight, join me on this journey.

Allow me to echo parts of your experience and perhaps lend words to the unspeakable. Let's hold hands as we climb together, into wholeness, into self-love and lasting sovereignty.

Let's open to the experience and be willing to feel everything. For to be safe we need to be whole, and being whole means standing strong in acceptance of all that we are.

These are the 100 steps I walked to find my way home...

the fall

100…

The weight in my chest is
sudden pulling me down
as decades of dreams fall

The room expands an echo
of the gulf between us
my gasping breath sharp
in the silence left by the
slammed door

The world becomes a blur
as I hold my breath
the tears mutiny and fall

I am lost unravelling
pieces of identity
alongside the plans
we created together

I press my back to the wall
seeking the support
you have pulled away
my legs shake as I fall

The ground meets me
its touch the opposite of
the quicksand I expect
as hope walks away

99…

The bitterness is raw
like bile in my throat
we imagined a life
yet you gave up and fled

I cannot leave
you've handed me
the broken pieces
crumpled and discarded
I stay, alone to repair

You walk out into freedom
mistakes in the past
a chance to begin again
the gift of redemption

I endured, I fought
and now a mountain to climb
the lone survivor
left to finish what we started

A seed of dark hate
twisted in and embedded deep
I will drag myself to the top
but who will I be when I arrive?

98…

Fight for me
I beg with my eyes
But silence stretches out
The space widening
A void I long to throw myself into

I want you to beg
To plead
To see what you are losing
Leap for me with desperate hope
Show me the love you've hidden
for so long.

97...

my throat is swollen
my lips clamped shut

I'm terrified if I open my mouth
all the pain will come rushing out

the world blurs behind a wall of tears
I will not let them fall.

96…

A relationship ending
is like the lights coming on
at the end of the night.
I close my eyes
willing for darkness to return
Hoping the truth will disappear.

95...

I wish you were dead

I wish the empty space was because you were taken rather than left

I wish I could mourn the loss of you with death's finality

I wish I could reminisce with grief's rose tinted gaze

I wish for closure

94…

I want to be free of this
I want to run away and start again
I want to fill my days with me

My creativity
My friendships
My self

I want to sleep and heal my body
I want to take time over my food
I want to soak the stress away

My escapism
My quiet
My peace

I want to talk on the phone
I want to laugh in person
I want my space

Why do you get to take that for yourself?
Why do you deserve what I yearn for?
Why do you not see me?

93…

The judgements my head makes
The words I imagine in your gaze
I am not that woman
the single mother
the forty something divorcee
only I never got married

Permanently tired
        Often frazzled
                Increasingly bitter

My smile is tight to hide the grief

I can't stop to chat
there's no one to pick up my slack
I'm not me any longer
there's no time for that
Just the forward motion
of the lives I'm responsible for
A cog in the watch that never stops

92…

Lonely and alone
Unwanted and incomplete
She's been abandoned
Half of the whole that has disintegrated
Single and unloveable
Left on the shelf
Without a partner
She's been discarded, disguarded.

91…

I can't beg you to stay when this was my idea
The 'right thing' that destroys a lifetime
                                        I ache

Somewhere deep down that was hidden and protected
A place of keening sounds and tearing sensations
                                        I want

I'm an adult who accepts that this isn't enough
Yet I fear this future I have instigated
                                      I crumple

I show strength and conviction
Knowing I'll need double to carry us through this
                                      I grieve

I miss the smile on your lips when you're not looking at me
The friend that I've lost, that huge part of me
I love you

endings

90...

My heart tells me it was only hours ago
Your goodbye still echoing on the air
Words hitting my spine as they cut through me

The truth is it's been months
You are a ghost in this space
A memory of fingertips on skin and breath intermingling

Do your thoughts stray to this place, to that time
As the dust falls through sunlight
Coating my body like a frozen kiss

89...

My heart is sore and heavy
it fills my chest and belly
my whole body has become heart
throbbing and aching and stark
it drowns out my thoughts
I exist only in this:

                    suspended in loss

88…

I'm scared
This broken thing offers safety
Familiarity giving me a place to hide
Shrinking from the unknown
Both the failure and the hope
Torment me

Your arms are like my own
Your presence a reliable comfort
I am terrified of the empty space
The echoing hole
The forced realisation
I am alone.

87…

There's a space in the bed
Cold sheets
Unused pillows
A mattress that never moves
Your weight isn't there
No breath but my own

I stretch my limbs
I am not big enough
The space remains
It niggles at me like a forgotten word
It itches like staring eyes on my back
You are not here

86...

I gave you my heart
and watched as you cut it
into tiny, neat, slices

85...

My arms fall open
Hands ready to accept the blow you prepare to unleash
My throat closes
Trapping my words within
So much I yearn to say
So much I need you to understand
Yet I stand in motionless silence

The shape of your shoulders
Protective and resolute
I am behind you now
A shadow on the floor that you move out of
The soft click of an apologetic door
It wanted no part of this finality
The quiet fills the expanding space

You have taken more than your body
More than a toothbrush and some clothes
You've stolen the air
Bleached all colour
Turning me into a faded photograph
A forgotten snapshot of your past
A muted memory

84…

Sometimes I burn with indignatious rage,
Sometimes I choke on all the words I have not spoken,
I struggle to swallow them down
One. More. Time.

I can't speak with your hands across my mouth,
teaching me to hold my tongue.
I can't move with you always in front of me,
teaching me to know my place.

My mind is kept full of meaningless news,
My hands kept busy with monotonous drudgery,
I am occupied,
I am unable to free myself.

It bubbles and boils,
It burns through my veins,
races with my thunderous heartbeat,
surges within my chest,
threatening to explode out on my breath.

My rage is righteous,
It is the glitter in my eyes,
the heat in my stare,
the fuel I survive on.

83...

There's something stirring
Deep within
In a voiceless place
Where certainty lives
Words on the tip of my tongue
Close enough to taste
Memories just out of reach
A vision on the periphery
Sensations in my body
A vibration in my cells
The echo of me
Refusing to stay buried

82…

What if, what if, what if?
A voice whispers an idea
As fragile as a spider's lace
What if I could do this?
What if I could be okay?
The flutter of a bird's wing
As it attempts flight
Uncertainty
The fear of falling deeper into the dark

But, what if, what if, what if?
The breeze urges
Tugging at my hair
Demanding attention
The voice is skittish
Dancing along the edges
Like a fairy tale being
Unwilling to be seen

So, what if, what if, what if?
Flirting with my consciousness
As in the moments between light and dark
The moments before the dawn
When the light returns
And shows us the way home

81...

As night covers us
The barriers melt away
And we turn to each other
Bodies speaking what our voices cannot
The darkness helps us hide
An enabler to our avoidance
Children and jobs
Work and money
Petty resentments
Unspoken slights

As night steals away sight
The weight of a gaze filled with need
Overflowing with hurt
Searching for answers to silent questions
It restores my hearing
Each sigh of breath and rustle of sheets
The suspended hours between the bustle of life
Touch becomes communication
Our hands cross a divide our voices cannot
Stripped back to sensation
Shields abandoned as we rejoin
Will it be enough to help us travel through tomorrow's light?

questioning

80...

Could I hand you the keys to my home
To every locked door
And every secret within?

Could I offer you the knowledge of my past
The story of every scar
And every aching wound?

Could I reveal myself to you
Uncover all my layers
And stand naked to your eyes?

Could I let you hear my stories
Truths I dress in beautiful lies
And hide even from myself?

Could I trust my instincts ever again
To know where I am safe
And loved?

79...

The kiss of light
turning black to grey

dawn is a realm of possibilities
the edge of a beginning

78…

When did I stop loving you
When did desire die out and habit take over
When did the monotony of life seep into us
and fill the growing cracks
When did routine cloud our eyes
And we forget how lucky we were

When did my rock become a boulder on my path
And when did I take up a hammer and chisel
When did I forget I was made of water
And that I could flow through and flow past

When?

77...

Did a wave of sadness ever hit you
Striking with surprise
Filling your mouth with saltwater tears?

Did your knees ever give way
As you stumbled on the path
So determined to be strong but unable to deny your soft centre?

Lean in
Lean in to the grief, the loss and the heartache
Surrender to the swells that want to wash you away
Bow your head in acknowledgement
Of all the stories that have made you
And with a deep breath
Stand once more

76…

It's not the hunger of passion
or the initial urgency to know you
it's the familiarity and comfort of knowing someone
the wreathing together of decades rendering words unnecessary
It's love in eyes and hands
It's everything I pretended we had
But the lights are on
The truth is stark

75…

There is darkness around me that you helped to create
Our dance wove a spell rich in curses and villains
The darkness inside is mine alone
The poison of jealousy dripping like acid
Corroding love that began so invincible
Possession and envy tangled and suffocating
Squeezing out every last tear of compassion
Bitterness and resentment bubbling in the pot
Their taste and smell overpowering everything else
Coiling together, intertwining and inseparable
My belly is full and writhing
I can set you free but what of me?

74...

I want something I don't have language for
Something that deviates from the known path
Something only found when we leave safety behind

I want the security of love
Without the sniper fire of logistics and frustration
I want the receptivity of friendship
Without the exhausted indifference of complacency

I want the spark of conversation
When we haven't shared every waking moment
I want touch that feels like coming together
After separation

I want the old you
Before you drowned under the weight of life
I want the old us
When we had enough love left over for each other

The you that still survives
Smiling at me from time to time
The us that holds on by fingertips
The flaking glue to this creation

I don't know the how
But I know the what
Is it enough for a first step?

73...

If I met you now, I wonder
But didn't I meet you everyday
Or did I stop seeing the person in front of me
Did I stop noticing your subtle changes

If I could turn back time, I wonder
But wasn't I there for every moment
Or did I fall asleep along the way
And stop living the life I had dreamt of

If I could hear the answers
Whispered down over the years
I would know that when I turned my back on me
The loss of you was promised to follow

You loved me when I was wild and free
Alive with passion that overflowed
But now I have returned
Gold in the cracks and spirit on fire
Eyes wide open
Here I am

72…

A shaft of light
Dust mites swirling
Here I stand
Bathed in hope
I can't see fear
But I can see myself
Light kisses my skin in greeting
Offering me a reminder of warmth
The first steps home.

71...

Some days I wake to power flowing up my spine
Lifting my chest
My gaze to the sky

Some days I wake deflated
As though a night creature had pulled the plug
And my spirit drained away in the dark

Facing another day
Overflowing with things I can't muster a smile for
Unable to hear the whispered possibilities
A part of me still believes in

I carry that fragment delicately cradled in my palms
Just a sliver of soul light to protect
Until she rises again

grief

70…

I dwell in a cave that was borne from the waves
Water flowing, pushing against rock
Rubbing against stone and finding its way

Wave upon wave beating against me
In urgent violent swells and gentle ebbs and flows
Soothing the abrasions

Grief comes pounding, knocking me off my feet
Then the gentle swells rock me to sleep

Anger comes rushing fast
Filling the space, stealing all air
Until it is pulled away again in its ceaseless journey

Sadness comes as the spray jumps high
So high I cannot escape it
As it chokes my throat
The rough walls steady me

The darkness of this space
Blinding my eyes yet opening my heart
Freeing me from thought
Submerging me in sensation

The water has hollowed the rock
As my tears have emptied me
I ride the waves
As they carry 'I' back to 'me'

69...

I don't want you here
I like you gone
When the only you is one of my imagination

I hold conversations in my head
Weave fantasies of your return
It's a fiction I can hide in

Lying close to the truth
Inspired by real life
Glimpses drawn of a future to the fullness of its possibility

You return
And with the opening of a door
The dream closes

Illusions disintegrating
Fading from memory
Like whispered promises.

88...

I'm scared
This broken thing offers safety
Familiarity giving me a place to hide
Shrinking from the unknown
Both the failure and the hope
Torment me

Your arms are like my own
Your presence a reliable comfort
I am terrified of the empty space
The echoing hole
The forced realisation
I am alone.

67...

Knives don't do this
The sharp, cold, metal of a blade slices quickly and cleanly
Love does this
Gouging, twisting, hollowing you out
A part of you is missing
A wound too wide and deep to ever fully disappear

66...

They say that time heals all wounds
But time cannot separate me from you

I move around our empty house
Your echo following my every step
I feel your breath upon my neck
your voice whispering your needs

we had a lifetime
before the gold tarnished
repetition dulls and fades
the sparkle of what once was
now sounds are hollow
I am the only one left

They say that time is limitless
But we ran into its wall of stone
I carry you within me
But outside I am alone

I stand in the doorway
Open space at my back
Closed, I touch its wood
Still warm from the dying sun

The night has come
I will walk into the dawn once more.

65...

I met someone new tonight
A glimpse in a crowded room
And later when our eyes met in a reflection

I felt someone new tonight
A presence I couldn't deny
And a brush against my body waking up my senses

I heard someone new tonight
A voice of conviction
And a message I wanted to listen to

I danced with someone new tonight
A confident sensuality
And an ownership of a body that held no shame

I touched someone new tonight
A soft sigh of surrender
And an intimacy I have longed for

I laughed with someone new tonight
A celebration of life and possibility
And a deep abiding freedom

Someone new with an old face
A version of me hidden in the dark
Are you ready to meet her too?

64...

What if you can't love me the way I want to be loved?
What if I shouldn't settle?
What if you were mine for a reason, a season and a lifetime?
What if our lifetime has come and gone?

What if ours was only one song?
What if another is starting?
What if you are perfect?
What if you are not supposed to be mine?

What if we change and learn and grow?
What if we have to say goodbye?
What if the people we are now can find each other?
What if we are our new beginning?

What if I'm strong enough?
What if I can make a decision?
What if I can take a leap for us both?
What if I can trust love to lead our way?

63…

Taken for granted
I am the unseen but expected
Dependable and reliable
Compliments offered like lashes
Always here
To be trusted
Arms forever open
Body willing
Until it's not

62...

I have become invisible
Yet I make myself bigger than ever
You cannot see me
As I hide in plain sight
I muffle my voice
Around the food I suffocate my pain with
Pushing the screams down
Keeping my silence
I get bigger and bigger
Yet you notice me less
So big you can't see me at all.

*here in
the quiet*

61...

My heart isn't big enough
To fill this silence

60…

Night falls and the dark creeps in
Body sinking into soft folds I close my eyes
There behind my eyelids
Are the razor sharp memories of us
The bruises inside my chest
Born from goodbyes and hidden from the day
Motion, chatter, and a smiling mask
All tools to push away the ache
That here in the quiet
I cannot outrun

59...

When you breathe to a metronome
How do you find your own rhythm?

In the night time stillness
A solitary heartbeat echoes in the dark.

58...

What you sign up for is rarely
what you get.
Question is, are the lessons,
the experience worth it?

57...

I gave you all the power
You hold the control
I follow your lead
In this dance to your tempo
I wait for your call
The decisions are all made by you
I juggle and wait
At war with myself
I push back shame with anger
A righteous indignant rage
White hot and boiling
The thud of another bar
In the barrier I am building
A new boundary
Defences that will withstand
That will keep the threat out
And prevent a weak surrender
I am reclaiming the power
I am taking back control
I am changing the tempo
And I am making the call.

56…

The loneliness creeps in at the strangest times
Reaching under your ribcage
Pinching at the soft hidden parts you thought you had protected
All the moments are filled with you

Your smell
     Your sound
          Your presence

Memories of the past chasing me through my day
I school my face and straighten my crown
But I carry us everywhere

55...

When I'm alone
I weave the empty room
Creating a fantasy of tantalising comfort
I imagine an us with you loving me
Longed for words falling unprompted
Acknowledgements and culpability
Intimate truths and word caresses

When you are here
The room is full
The emptiness grows in the hidden spaces
Leaving no room for fantasy
The loneliness is sharp
The truth brutal
I twist to turn away from it

A void of intimacy
No words of love or care
No connection that bonds us
Nothing but empty space
As you fill my world
But inhabit your own

54…

I hold her hand gently
As I lean in close
Whispering softly
It will not be okay
This scrabbling in the dark
Not be okay
This journeying in the dark

You will stumble and fall
Reopening old wounds
You will slip as the ground moves beneath you
And you try to find safety
You will feel weary
As the path remains uphill
You will lose hope
As you struggle to keep going

The cracks in the darkness will appear
I say with urgency
Holding her hand tighter
There is a path
I need her to understand
Searching her gaze for hope
It will not be okay
But you will survive it

53...

every time I think I miss you
i see you and realise I don't

i miss being loved

52...

I am the tragic woman
The long suffering victim
The hard done by
The abandoned
The weary and the grief stricken
If I am not that story
What is left?
Do I need those narratives
To make you view me with kind eyes
To make you stay
Do I need to dress myself as a caricature
To huddle in false security

I am repeating words that are not mine
Words that craft a lens
An image shaped from half truths
Not trusting what I cannot control
The fear that I am not enough
That you won't stay for this alone
Yet as my own vision clears
I step away from influencing yours
I am enough
I gift myself the security of truth
As I allow the real story to be told

51...

Manipulator you yell
I fight the label as it tightens around me
Negative connotations ensnaring me
A mirror I long to smash

Manipulator I hear echo
Stalking me through my day
I twist and turn
I try to dismiss you and laugh it away

Manipulator I whisper
To my reflection late at night
I know the truth
But in your pain you never questioned why

50…

Holding on to a life raft
I forgot that I can float

reaching in

49...

We're made to share
We seek connection
So being alone hurts

We numb, distract and avoid
Taking our fix from the shallow waters of social media
Trying to replace what once lived beside us

I'm learning how to be alone
To share with myself
To connect with myself

No one taught me to reach in instead of reaching out

48…

Is the you I miss so much
a creation of my own making
or the reality of who you once were

Am I holding us to a fantasy
a possible version
existing in some alternate place

A place far from here
before betrayal left a trail of bruises
and harsh words withered our roots

Would I rather colour my sight with hope
sacrificing the present for dreams grown from potential
Do I dare face us as we are today

Can I allow the light in
to capture this moment and flood it with truth
Do I dare?

47...

Licking along the edges
whispering promises of transformation
turning solid wood to crumbling ashes
heat that can comfort or threaten
your fire has long grown cold
a memory of the night before
of good times past
my fire is just kindling
I surrender and allow it to consume me
as yours once did
this time it will last

46...

The old me flaked off as I scrubbed
skin reddening under the pummel of hot water
washing the stains of tears away
water rushing over my head
weighing down my hair
just as the memories weigh down my heart

45...

The hand on my back is lighter now
I think I can stand
The hand over my mouth is looser now
I think I can speak

As I stumble
Knees bloody
To my feet
I see with a clarity that is new

The spectre of you
Created by me
Is a vapour
Made solid by me

There is no supplication here now
I bow only to honour myself
There is no trading my needs for yours
I deserve happiness, now.

44...

Which of us has changed?
Which of us has become something they weren't
Something the other cannot meet halfway
Time and experience moulding our faces
Altering our personalities in a thousand small ways
When you live up close you don't notice
Hairline cracks become fissures
Wide enough to disappear into
Which of us fell in?

43…

jaw aching
head pounding
lids like sandpaper against my eyes
I've been dreaming of you again

42...

I'm not broken
I'm just hurt
an animal trapped in a snare
begging for help
unable to receive it

41...

I thought I was enough for both of us
Turns out I'm enough for me.

40…

Time keeps moving
It does not stop for grief
It does not pause for confusion
There is no time to catch your breath
No time to patch up a bruised heart

Time keeps moving
Days blur into months, then years
Thirties turn swiftly into forties
The future comes rushing past
As I watch numb, on the side lines

Time keeps moving
I don't recognise my life
This was not the plan
The path looked very different
I have lost my way and I can't turn back

Time keeps moving
I try to catch up
Regaining momentum
On feet that are new
I can't be left behind

Time keeps moving
I find the pace
A pulse restarted
A heart brought back to life

surrender in strength

39…

I am descendent of queens and fae
Crying out for support I forgot how to accept
Gathering the shreds of discarded dreams
Now is the time to begin anew

I am descendent of queens and fae
Willing myself on through the dark
I stand a little taller, walk a little faster
Learning to love and hope
Learning to surrender in strength

I am descendent of queens and fae
My journey is long and far from over
Under my skin lies the power of generations
Stories to be lived through and shared
The path ahead is a winding one but I step
With certainty and trust

38...

The first step is blind, a stumble as your hands
Grope along the wall the panic sets in

The second is fuelled by fear desperation quickly follows
The idea of being stuck here lost in this darkness
Alone and abandoned

The third step is quick then comes resolution
You are not supposed to be here this is not your place
Your foot comes down more solidly as you begin to remember

The fifth step is a crossroads the path splits before you
Do you try again or try for yourself?
You call it a pause for breath but it's a moment of gathering
Pulling in your hope and faith
Weighing them against your worth and strength

The path begins to slope it's so easy to slip back
When you're on an uphill climb you have to want every step
Some days you march others you just try to stand still
The darkness you've come from, a comfort
A place to lie down and surrender
The light ahead an exposure
Full of noise, people and disappointment
Your heart wants to duplicate
To run in both directions
Faith keeps you moving
Slowly forward.

37...

My fantasy life has taken a turn
I'm not sure what it means
My eyes drink in pictures of families
Laughter on their faces
Their bonds so visible and strong
I wonder where ours went
When the laughter died
When the smiles faded
When it all became one long struggle

My fantasies feel out of reach
The stuff of my dreams
Yet the reality of other people
Kinder, wholesome, undamaged people
My eyes tell me it's possible
I want to learn so my children don't have to
So I watch them and their lives
Absorbing the possibility of home.

What would the image look like with just me
Can I remember to laugh and play
To fight the habits
The weight of responsibility
Tying my soul down
Exhausting my body
Consuming my thoughts
Can there be enough warmth and love
To hide the chill from where
You are supposed to be
Am I enough to hold the hearts of this family?

36…

A quickening
I want the whole world to pause
So I can feel this fragile flutter
The barest sensation of movement
A suggestion of hope

A quickening
I hold my breath scared to lose my connection
Deep within me
Stirring something forgotten
A whispered echo of a promise

A quickening
I am still alive
Tiny and vulnerable
Fighting on and worth fighting for
A proof of life

35...

Our breath intermingled
Creating a fog that blinded us
Holding hands we stumbled
Trusting the other to lead
To a destination unvoiced
The haze lifts
Our hands pull apart
We return to our unshared paths

34...

The surface seems too far above
The light faint as my lungs begin to scream
I desperately search
Looking for someone to help with this load
The weights pulling me ever downward
Fingers gripping tightly
Holding on to death as if to a life raft
I watch my hands as they drown me

Part of me kicks, fighting back
Against the fingers that won't let go
Deeper in and darker it gets
I can't do this much longer

The surface is but a pinprick of light
A distant star where hope and possibilities lie
Teasing in its presence
Should drops away
Duty follows, sinking fast into the depths

The image I've been carrying
The reflection I've been hoping to see
Faded with lack of light
Fingers now numb
Unable to hold onto anything
Releasing in surrender

All I had to do to rise
Was let go

33...

The air is thick
A storm is coming
My head aches
As the pressure builds
I turn my face to the sky

Bruised and swollen
Full to bursting
It will open soon
Holding back
But needing release
It is here, now

Wrenched open
Torn apart
Flowing in an unstoppable torrent
Pouring out
Covering everything it touches
Washing the debris away

Head back, eyes closed
Drinking it in
Granting it access
Allowing it to cleanse
To release the wild
That we echo in each other

I feel a power build
My diaphragm swells
My lips clamp shut
The swell increases
I am the keeper of a storm

Lips flung apart
A sound bursts out of me
Streaming forth
Filling the air with my wild

My sound, water's touch
Intermingle
Recognising each other
Unleashed
Unbound
Torn open
Wild.

32…

The blood drops
I watch it leave me
A shedding

In its red tint
The shame flows away
My failings depart

Like a skin I no longer need
An image that wasn't mine
Discarded and let go

The blood flows
A part of me leaves
The part that smothered the rest

Its dark colour
The old stories
My body ready for a new narrative

Beliefs I wore like protection
Embroidered with barbs
Falling away as I step free

The blood carries away the past
Emptying me
Creating space
For the me still standing

31…

         I stand up

      Vertebrae by vertebrae

        I stand tall

   Unwilling to curl in on myself

    I will take up space

  As I make the daily climb

To be visible

30...

I am awake
Skin alive with sensation
My body feline
Soul rooted and connected

I am awake
Skin responding to touch
Air kissed and supported as I lie exposed
Self-embodied and present

I am awake
Skin supple and glistening
My hands responding to my needs
Owning the whole of me

I am awake
My body to please
No waiting or asking
Now I am both giver and receiver

29…

I can hear the difference
Feel the opposing resonance of my thoughts and feelings
Thoughts that stumble and often lie
Thoughts that belong to a different time
To your 'me'
The me that held on
Glossed over
And made pretty pictures out of mud

Feelings are vague and often hard to define
Feelings are beneath the surface
They belong to this me
The me that got quiet enough to hear
That took the time to learn the language
The truth that my body always knew
That the pictures I create deserve the brightest colours

quiet certainty

28...

Quiet certainty
Puzzle pieces slot together
Broken parts remoulded
It is not a return
Something new
Barely formed
Just beginning
Wordless still
Without clear direction
But stronger
More solid
And growing
With quiet certainty

27…

I never wore a veil for you
But I hid my eyes
I maintained a shadow of myself
A mask that shifted with time

My veil was self-inflicted
A permanent disguise
Forgotten in its familiarity
A betrayal that cemented lies

A veil that blanketed me in fog
To stop me from being seen
A mist over a mirror
A world behind a screen

The time has come to raise the veil
And meet my own eyes
To uncover all my truths
And heed their hidden cries

I never wore a veil for you
That path was not mine to walk
I am ready now to be visible
And be the hero that I sought

26…

Little me, I'll hold you close
it's going to be alright
Little me, set down your fears
I'll keep you safe from harm.
Little me, release your grip
you can let go, it's safe to fall
Little me, I'm so sorry
your needs weren't met at all.
Little me, now is the time
to embrace the truth of today
Little me, you are just one aspect
but I am here to stay.
Little me, I love you
you are worth more than he could ever say
Little me, don't let the doubting voices
stand in your way.
Little me, you were the princess
locked in a tower of need
but little me,
I am the Queen who was one day freed.
Together we are strong
and our truth cannot be hidden
we will never need their validation
or anyone's permission.
From this moment let's go forward
together, hand in hand
Little me, it's time to make a stand.

25…

I've been chasing down an image
That the world helped me to create
An idealised version of what life could be
That stayed always out of reach
The years have faded what was once so clear
A sepia photograph
I've tried to mould us
I've bent the light
Twisted worlds and woven illusions
All to keep us going, reaching for the impossible
The dream is not wrong
But the players have been badly cast
Not everything is meant to be
And not everything can last
We danced our dance and shared our time
We taught each other well

But now that faded image must be discarded
Allowing us to rest
A new one drawn by hand
An acceptance that this wasn't ours
So I release you with love
I'm sorry I made you stay
It wasn't that you were wrong
Just that our life wasn't supposed to go that way
You've been my partner and companion
On a journey so winding and long
I could not have made it here without you
But this is the end of our song.

24…

I'm missing something and it's not you
It's the solid ground I used to stand on

The knowing where I am
And who I am now that I stand alone

I am a swirling mass without a centre
Trying to settle and reform

I built a world around you
Upon a dream of a shared life

Breathing into the loss and pain
I find my first foothold in the foundations

I will build a castle of truths
With bricks of integrity, trust and love

As I clear my space on this ground
I will always know where I stand and who I am

23…

the blood comes
protecting me from myself
creating a barrier
that you won't want to pass

the blood comes
stopping your hands
stilling their path
forcing a different communication

the blood comes
i am reminded of my power
it stands between us
banishing my weakness

the blood comes
and I am more than my body
more than my need to hide in your arms
i am spirit, wind and fire

the blood comes
it returns me to myself
sensations heightened
I am home

22…

Breathing in the sea
Into the deepest parts of me
Down to the place my secrets hide
A dream waits for life

Drinking in the salt
Of eternal unshed tears
Soaking into the parched folds
A voice waiting to sing

Submerging myself in the waters
Washing away the grime
Revealing the undressed beauty
A woman ready to shine

21...

Grasp
Pull
Rise

Fumble
Slip
Rise

Through tunnels of mistrust
Through caverns of shame
I have climbed
Determined to be myself again

Fight
Struggle
Rise

Strive
Push
Rise

Through deliberate choice
Through daily commitment
I have climbed
And now I lie gasping on the surface

into the light

20…

I have needs
I do not fear voicing them
My words ring out
Clear of hesitation
Resounding with clarity
My body free
No longer muffled by confusion

I have needs
They are not yours to meet
Pleasing is not my priority
I want you to hear
Know the real me
Feel my conviction
See me stand

I have needs
I know my worth
I will honour myself
Celebrate my self
Thanking you
For the lessons I no longer require

I have power

19…

Body image like a coastline
Slowly eroding
Words like waves
Battering the shore

Alternating hot and cold waters
The scorch of your glare
The rub of your apathy
Wear me down

Like the moon
I can control the tides
Making barriers
Creating protection

I will conserve what is here
Appreciate what remains
Rebuild with gratitude
Restore my self
The beauty of nature can change
But not be destroyed by the hands of man

18…

If you want to kiss these lips
You should find them worthy of listening to.

17…

Here I am
Broken
But reformed
Unsure
Yet certain
Here I am

16…

My hands are open
Able to release you
Ready to receive all I am offered

My hands are open
No longer holding on
Ready to catch me if I fall

My hands are open
Fists uncurled I put down the fight
Ready to greet the future

My hands are open
No longer pushing life away
Ready to reach out in acceptance

I am open

15…

There are moments in the dark
When the loneliness is piercing
Moments that have me begging for the future to arrive today
When I'll be held in the dark
Secure and safe within the arms of another
Knowing that dawn is always faced together

In this moment I feel alone
The only arms to hold this weight are my own
The only arms to meet our needs
The only arms to bring us security

This loneliness isn't empty
It is full of all the strength and courage I carry
I am safe because I make myself so
I am secure because I know who I am

There will be a moment when I can rest
When another's arms will take my load
Until then
I am strong enough to hold my own

14…

There is clarity in silence
My voice has no one to compete with
I know what I want
And I am calling it to me

13…

A true king is a true leader
One who stands before his people
Rather than use them as a shield
One who serves their needs
Rather than demanding homage
One who protects the land
Rather than using it for his gain
One who seeks trust, respect and love
Rather than fear, duty and coercion
A man can call his love a queen
When he can look himself in the mirror
And know he is a king.

12...

I am the wind
I strip back the trees
I sweep the forest floor
I pull your hair
I push you back and forth
And scream 'wake up'
Change is here

11…

The ground has shifted
I know now that it is constantly flowing
Sometimes so slowly you barely noticed
Others rough, sharp and sudden
Toppling you over
Bringing you to your knees

I have shifted
What once flowed to fit the surroundings
Now has a centre, a core
Solid and unchanging
Safe in its consistency
I will move and grow
I will adapt and learn
But I will forever be the reclaimed
Me.

the fires ignite

10…

Pretty, pretty lies
The stories we weave
Fantasies of fairy tales
The magic lens we absorb the world through
Always wanting to believe
Desperate to retain hope
How will you recognise the real thing
When you dress the imposters so well?

9...

Engulfed in flames of change
White hot but pure
No good or bad present
Just the endless climb

I stand tall in my pyre
Welcoming the fuel you offer
Accepting the transformation
The fire licks away the old layers

Crackling skin is shedded
Falling into the ash at my feet
I breathe in the heat
Burning inside and out
Finally ready to rise

8...

Unmarried unwed
Unbound to another
I stand ready and waiting
Hand to heart and breathing
I vow

I vow to see me
In all of my truth
I vow to hear me
And all of my needs
I vow to touch me
Deep, where my softest self hides

I vow to honour
The journey I have taken
I vow to cherish
The body that brought me here
I vow to obey
The voice inside

Married and wed
Bound to myself
I stand ready and waiting
Hand to heart and breathing

7…

The fires are burning
The womens' feet are pounding
A primal beat on the earth's surface
The moon is rising
A cool wash to meet my burning skin
I am lit from within
Dancing bright
Not the flame of rage
But an unbridled excitement in my belly
A warmth that radiates from my heart
A crackling that bursts from my throat
A night song of joyous tears
The fires are burning and I am home

6...

I hear my children's voices
Whispering down to me from their futures
Do you remember?
When mum did...
When mum took us...
When mum went...
I can, I am the one crafting these tomorrow stories
These shared memories
That will bind them
That will shape them
Inform them of what is possible
Lay the pathways they will find it easiest to walk
Their whispers begin strong
Yet fade before I hear the truth of my legacy
Unwritten, a work in progress
A work I stand aware of and grounded by
I will fill their mouths with greatness
Adventures that bring starlight shining in their eyes
Laughter to their tone and warmth to their bones
They will know courage
Faith in themselves
And a belief in their limitless nature
I will fill our todays with my true self
So I will live within them always

5...

I rest in stillness
Eyes seeking out slivers of light in the darkness
Slow even breaths curl around me
The house sleeps

A heavy weight of knowing lies on my chest
This path is hard and shadowed
The journey treacherous
I must be steady to not stumble

So I wean myself slowly
Mile by mile the blisters heal
These new shoes get broken in
Broken and healed to strengthen

4...

Stitched
Woven
Sewn back together

Fragments reclaimed
Owned
Welcomed back to the whole

One me
Unified in acceptance
Belonging only to myself

3…

Sunlight touches the crown of my head
Its gentle graze like an unseen hand
Playing a game and tingling my scalp
Its touch turning my hair auburn
As it highlights the hidden gold
It carries a warmth
I'd long forgotten
Allowing me to pause and rest
Knowing I'm almost home

2...

A flame is not needed to light your way
When you stand in the light
Rage is not needed to fuel you forward
When you feel acceptance
Burning is not needed for transformation
When you love yourself

1…

Your name on paper
Flame licks the edges
Letters blacken
Writing curls as heat rises
My hand twists to hold on longer

I offer it to the air
Watching it lift
As the fire consumes
My breath exhales

A gust of regret
To push it on its way
As it turns in on itself
Disintegrating to ashes
A ghost loose on the breeze

O...

I am Adeola
born of women strong
supported by women powerful
empowered by women wise

I am Adeola
a voice
a body
a beautiful spirit
and an ancient soul

I am Adeola
Student
Creator
Survivor
Queen

I have made the climb
I stand bathed in my light
I have returned
I am Home

CLIMBING IN THE DARK

Whether your heart aches from loss, betrayal or invisibility, the well of darkness that we can fall into has similar slippery walls and hidden pathways. A labyrinth of doubt, confusion and isolation, the journey back to the light of day can feel so long, so impossible, that just the act of trying can seem too much.

The bottom of my cavern was somewhere I never imagined myself reaching, but even from that place I knew that somewhere above me there was a shower of stars falling in the darkness, reminding me that there is always light and sometimes a little darkness is the catalyst to finding it.

It's not the darkness that scares us but being lost and severed from ourselves. The darkest parts of relationships are often the moments in which you realise you have strayed from who you really are. The moments when your eyes seem to clear, and you wonder at the life you see around you, a life that was never supposed to be yours.

You may stumble on the climb, you may need to pause and rest, you may reach moments in which you are sure you cannot take another step, but your inner voice is the torchlight in the dark and it is always there no matter how buried.

There is a window between the darkest part of night and the first glimpses of dawn, a stillness that holds all the potential of a new day. Live in that space and take into yourself the knowledge that with each rise of the sun, you too can rise.

Make your own light.

A.x

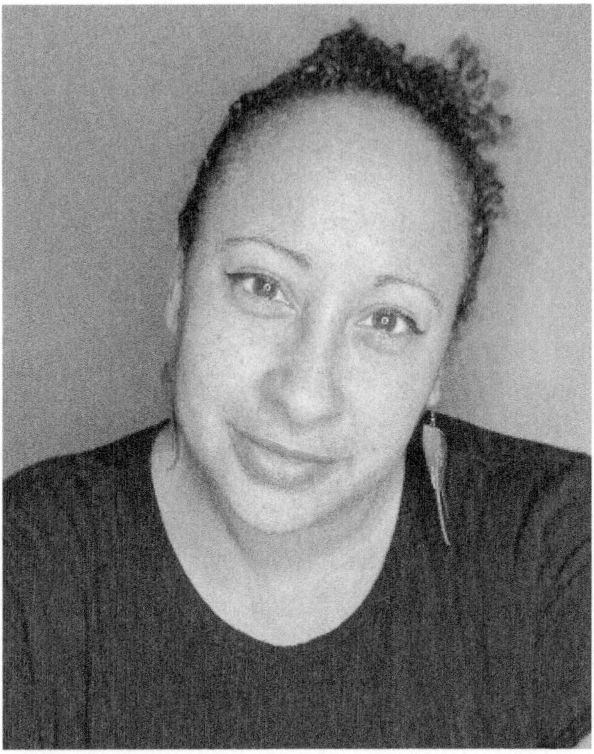

about the
AUTHOR...

ADEOLA SHEEHY is an Irish/Nigerian Londoner now living in the New Forest, with her four home educated children. Writing from the crossroads of race, womanhood, and creativity she uses prose to tackle the questions her mind ponders most and poetry to express the feelings closest to her heart.

Her experience as a yoga teacher and reiki master are at the root of her goal to encourage others through her words to live a fuller, more aligned life.

She is a columnist for The Green Parent magazine and has her own publication on Medium called The Honest Perspective.

You can find her work at the links below...

instagram @*adeola_moonsong*
website *adeolasheehy.com*

Climbing in the Dark Copyright © 2022 by Adeola Sheehy-Adekale.

All rights reserved. No part of this publication may be reproduced, distributed, or transmitted in any form by any means, including photocopying, recording, or other electronic methods without the prior written permission of the author, except in the case of brief quotations embodied in reviews and certain other non-commercial uses permitted by copyright law.

For permission requests, write to the author at adeolasheehy@hotmail.com or visit https://www.adeolasheehyaworldinwords.com/

ISBN: 978-1-80068-781-3

Design and Typesetting: Laura Lewis
Cover Image: Patrick Hendry @worldsbetweenlines

Printed in Great Britain
by Amazon